Rosewater

Siena Mellor

Copyright

First Edition
ISBN: 979-8-9884583-4-0

Love A Wholistic Life, Inc.

Dedication

For the hopeless romantics and the ones who find romantics hopeless.

Contents

Preface

Hello, I'd like to start off by saying thank you to the person holding *Rosewater* right now. The copy currently grasped in your hands is the physical manifestation of my hopes, dreams, fears, and ideals. The fact that you've purchased this means that my heart and soul matter. While some in my life say the only validation I need is my own, I happen to place a much higher value on the thoughts of my audience. I find that if I want to know that I am worthy, I need a new voice with new words to tell me, not an echo chamber of my own opinions.

As a general statement, this collection of my poems, essays, and smatterings of artwork are *mostly* derived from the experience of love. The same dead horse most poets kick. That oh-so familiar heartstring ripping muse that has followed artists of all walks for millennia. I suppose I have joined their ranks due to the fact that I am possessed by it as assuredly as the next day rises.

However before you flick through with expectations set by red roses and blue violets, I would also like to note that alongside my musings regarding infatuation and heartbreak my mind occasionally also spills over in other flavors of human existence. Yes, you will find Romeo and Juliet's likeness in these words and yes, you will also find their tragedy, (though not as dead as the horse), but you will also find my iterations of the wonders of this earth, despair, and delight. Things that make my soul sing lyrics other than love songs.

Luckily, (or perhaps unluckily), you will not find cordial nonsense within the bindings of this book. If you picked her up in hopes of finding clouds of fluffy poems I feel I must apologize now, as my work has never been composed with the intention to soothe, nor sugarcoat. I admit that I am bristling and utterly morbid at times, soft and sickeningly sensitive others. These pages are as human as I in my mind, a living breathing organism; and like anything alive she bleeds, wails, and wounds just as she may also nourish, whisper, and heal. A dual being like many.

It is my hope that you will find something meaningful within the artful confines of these pages and grasp onto it, because if you are to take anything from what I say here it is simply to never let go of what matters.

Rosewater

Poems

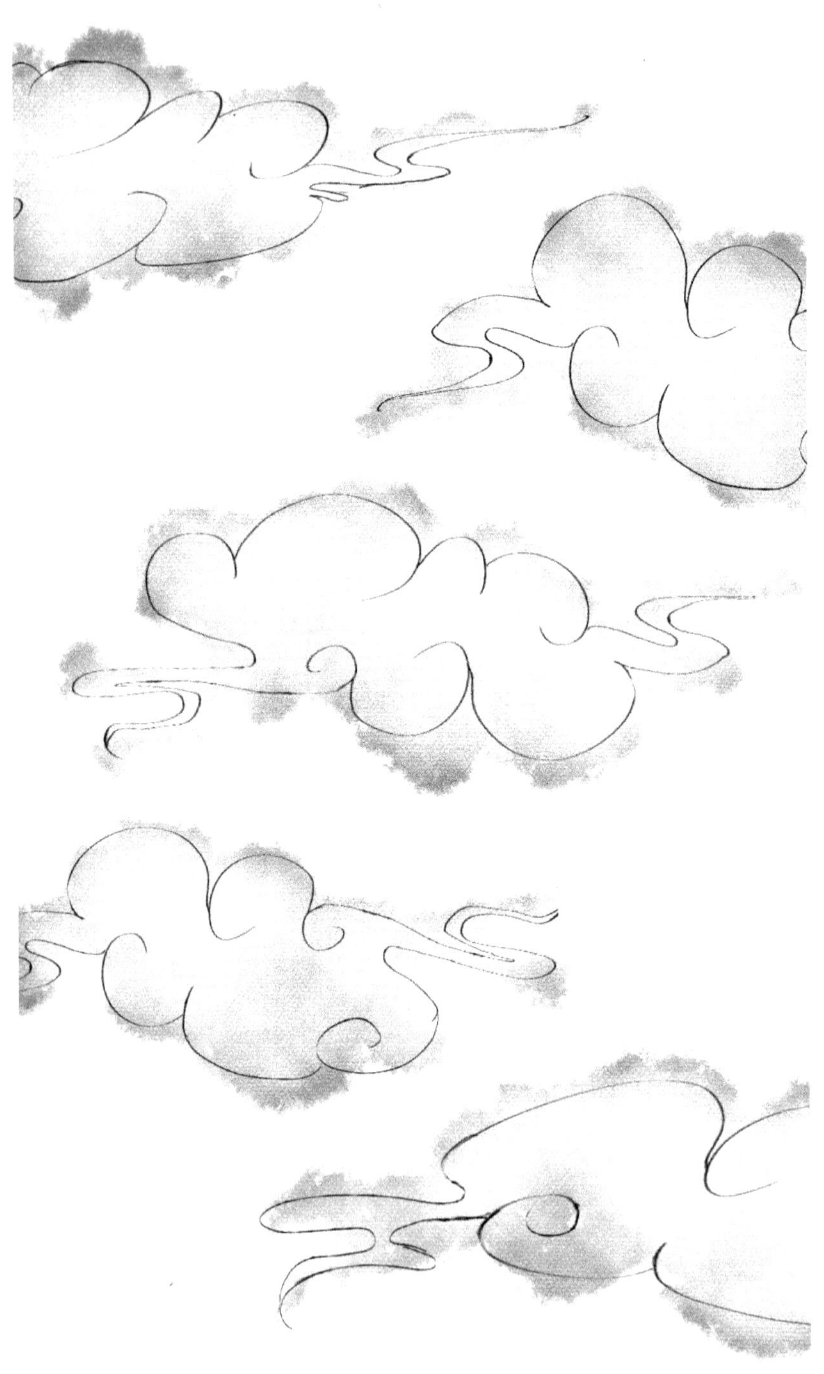

Grey.

I awoke the next morning to slicked ground and cold skies.

There's evidence of new gloom and rain present behind the drying streaks on my window,

The wind tosses and turns in the remnants of despair,

The trees and surrounding growth silently take the brunt of its force.

Uncomplaining, but unwilling

A certain silent sufferance.

It is Enough.

Closing my eyes

I sleep and dream that you love me

And I smile because

I can believe it is real

This soft wish within my bedsheets,

Slowly waking up

I remember the harsh reality

And I roll my eyes

As I roll over

Going back to sleep, going back to you.

Just like I always do.

Bloodied Fruit.

I hold the fruit of my heart gently
Once nestled deep inside the cavity of my ribcage waiting, it now beats in open air held by my outstretched palms.

Exposed.
Naive.
Hopeful.

The scent of ripe flesh carried by the wind to one who wishes to taste it
I've carved it from my chest just for you my dear, you're sure to be careful with a soft thing such as this.

Demure.
Fragile.
Trusting.

I wonder what my heart feels like in your hands as you raise it to your lips
Your fingers coated in the sticky-sweet of this affection, trickling slowly down the valley of your palms to the floor.

Saccharine.
Enticing.
Tender.

Your teeth tear into the fruit of my devotion
letting the nectar coat your tongue as you devour what you can, syrupy fluid dripping from the corner of your mouth as you swallow.

Carnal.
Cloying.
Crimson.

As you wipe the bloody dribble from your chin and sigh
I can only hope that I have satisfied you, feeding all that I am to bared fangs within shy smiles.

Waiting as I extend my hands once more, to feast upon your heart in return.

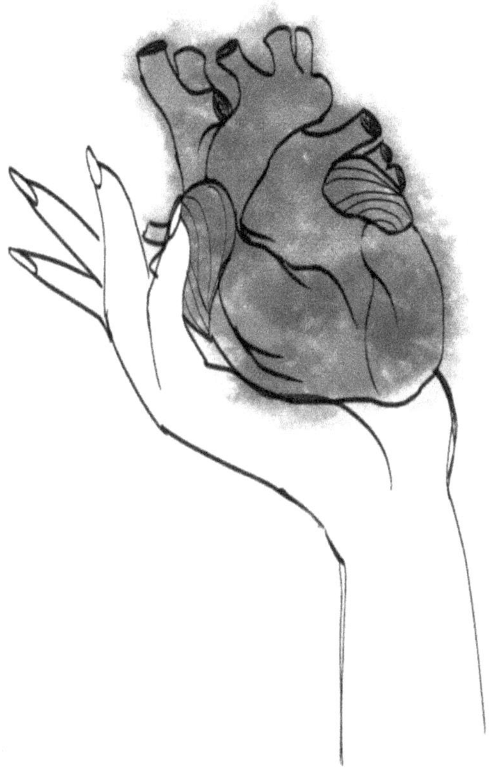

Botany.

Feeling is getting to me.

All the anxiety, sorrow, and rage I've kept stamped under dirt within the depths of my pelvis have finally begun to curl their way out of the earthen coffin I so lovingly provided them.

All at once I can feel dark brambles of sensitivity subtly pierce my innards. There is no blood, no physical harm, but the pain is beyond bearable.

Thorns softly shred their path through my stomach, my intestines, my uterus, (a gift that my mother says will never stop giving no matter how many times I beg it to.)

Briars thoughtfully tear their way up my sides and wrap into my ribcage, nestling the sharp odds and ends into my heart and lungs, my breath coming in shudderingly short and my sentiments leaking through in imperfect unpredictability.

Nettles sprout their familiar urticating up my spine and through my vertebrae. The sting setting my nerves alight with bitterness, nesting into my marrow like weeds left unchecked in the brush.

This sachet of seeds has been scattered by the hands of circumstance,

Rosewater

My once personable garden made beautiful with carefully cultivated flora I forced to bloom long out of their season has finally faced its reckoning. The invasive overgrowth of emotionally native pain.

It was by my hands and their superficial touch this perfectly curated greenhouse came to life and it is by my same hands' neglect of the imperfect within it that the glass is shattered and the growth within turned untamable and gruesome.

There are no shears strong enough to prune this piece of me out.

Detritus.

Leaves that fall
Like silent tears from a lonely child
Drift to the floor.

Nestled in open graves among their decaying brothers and sisters.
Corpses lying among the weak and sickly
The soon-to-die.

I wonder if the leaves can ponder their fate when they perch comfortable and green in the height of their trees. An open-air home, a brief safe haven for the youthful furls of life.

I wonder if they perceive the rot and decay just a few feet below them. Do they fear their inevitable descent into the thousands of others that came before?

I'd ask, only to be met with silence, standing amongst their detritus.

Rosa Sin Spinis.

A rose without thorns is like a love without tragedy.

Altered.
Fake.
Superficial.

If I reach out to grasp the stem and do not come back with blood smeared on my palm then I refuse to grasp it at all.

I do not believe in care without strife, adoration without abhorrence, one without the other is meaningless. How can one appreciate the delicate petals without the pain of punctured fingertips?

To crave unwavering devotion without the loss of sacrifice is selfish. Sharing your heart requires an understanding of the hardship that will follow.

Call me what you will,

A pessimist.
A masochist.
A cynic.

But please, do not brand me a liar for what I say.

Every rose has its thorns and every love has its pain. It is the way of the heart, the way of nature.

It is up to you whether or not you will accept this, and reach out anyway. Whether or not you will reach out and find your palms bloodied and your arms around another.

Rosewater

Astrophysics.

The earth revolves around the sun

and the moon pulls the tides.

This has been the way of the universe since it's dawning, the sun the galaxy's centerpiece and the moon the sea's.

I feel that human infatuation mimics this cosmic pattern. If stardust pumps life through our veins, may it not also pump love?

From orbits to tides to your eyes, there are coincidental comparisons I cannot help but draw.

By mere presence alone, your glow demands attention, the bright rays of something solar left highlighting the curvature of your face, your every ministration molten, left to flare in your wake. It is no wonder the earth orbits the sun, the force of your gravity will always draw my steps closer, my form a meager comportment in comparison, simply a planet honored to indulge in the warmth emanating from your iridescence. Earth's flora blooms seeing the sunlight just as my smile does when I see you.

Your golden nature eclipses with your silver speech, Still celestial in every right.

Like the moon's pull upon the ocean's swells, your gaze draws the tides of my heart up to shore, stirring the warm currents in my blood that brings red to my cheeks when you speak. Raging rushes brought about by even the most inconsequential of conversations... waxing waning, high flow to low, like fish on hooks I am hung on every word, though unlike them I'd have it no other way. Not when I am matching the sea's pace in trailing after you. I become reduced to sighs of seafoam and a heartbeat crashing like waves while you remain the epitome of lunar refinement.

It is the cosmic chord of correlation I string together, a universal truth I mirror in the patterns of my pulse and you in the swirling of your fingerprints.

Infatuation becomes a retelling of the greatest rhythms of life.

Alveolar Osteitis.

My heart bleeds for you much like how gums bleed for lost teeth, ripped from their places with a harshness that seems inappropriate for something so small.

You were never small. You were always larger than life.
Filling my veins till bursting with warmth, bringing a rosy tint to my cheeks and to my eyes, bathing the world around me in fuzzy pink feelings.

My veins run blue now, my tongue running over the empty space in my mouth, irritating and rubbing raw the bloody hole you left behind. Refusing to let that ache heal, finding remnants of you in the bony fragments still remaining, and that sharp throbbing of my heart. Beating in time with your footsteps as you walk, not run, away from me.

Despite my bleeding, you ripped yourself from my side much unlike a tooth. Leaving with an indifference that seems inappropriate for something so big.

How I Live.

I breathe in a type of desire that burns going down, like smoke filling my lungs, clouding my mind and fogging my vision as it blows into my eyes, stinging them as I blink away the tears.

I'm addicted to this special brand of misery, my drug of choice. You asked me never to abuse a substance, to never ruin myself that way. I ask you now not to worry, my body will not atrophy with this form of escape, I am only destroying my heart. Allowing the tar of frequent indulgence to build up inside it, letting it ooze through my already sluggish blood.

Cannabis, heroin, ketamine, and cocaine. All of which people abuse and use. I find nothing in such empty pleasures, I have found nothing in most pleasure itself as of recent. It's become bland and tasteless.

My palate demands its melancholic opposite, the bitter-sweetness of memory and the present pain of it.

It's masochistic. It's pointless to those who enjoy the pleasurable slop plated to them as their lives. But I take my meals with harsh reality and coffee that burns my tongue like yours did.

And I can't forget the desire tucked in my pocket for later... ready to be lit, putting smoke back into my eyes.

Siena Mellor

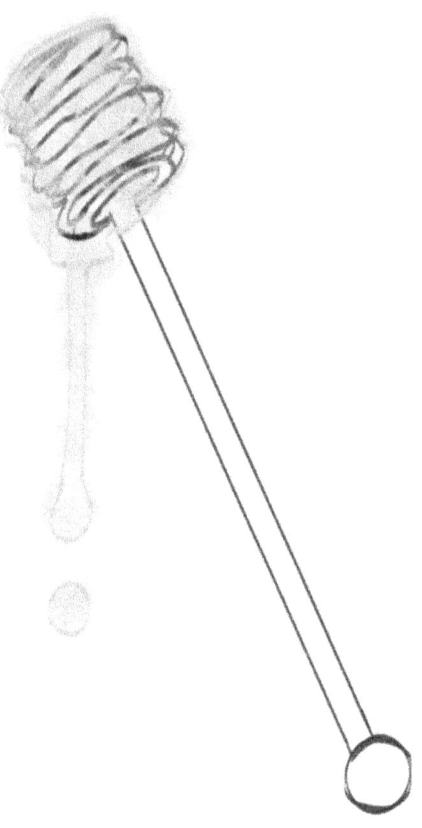

Sweet.

I can taste your tears on my lips,
Sweet and raw like honey.

But I'm only fooling myself as my tongue darts out to meet nothing but the empty air as what I know to be my tears streak down my face, slipping to the curve of my mouth.

It is cruel, but if I imagine hard enough I can still feel you, ghosting your touch on my skin, the tingling of your lips pressed against mine.

I can pretend that I'm kissing tears from the deep wells of your eyes, comforting you the way I long to be on the nights that my bones shake with loneliness and my mind relapses into memory.

But I am only fooling myself.

My tears taste bitter on my tongue, but if I just keep imagining that they belong to you, Honey, they taste sweet.

Refined Tastes.

I never liked black coffee. I always found it too bitter, the flavor lacking in depth. Call my pallet unrefined but any time I braved the liquid my senses revolted, I was decidedly someone who drank her sugar. Masking those harsh notes with cream, a pump of syrup or five to put my tongue at ease.

I'm not sure when my tastes began to change.

Maybe it started when I began drinking in your gaze instead of mochas. Marveling at how your irises swirled in the umber, so dark I could've sworn they were black. Only when the sun caught your eyes could you see the kaleidoscope of deep hues.

I started asking for less cream,

said I wanted to "taste the coffee"

I quit getting five pumps, easing down to one,

said I "didn't need all that sugar."

Maybe our leap from all to less to nothing translated to my taste buds too. I couldn't stomach all that warm sugar and milk, I was seeking a substitute to deep dark stares and found it in liquid tenebrae swirling in overpriced cups. Iced americanos replacing my usuals.

The color is enough to satisfy some nostalgic part of me. Even as the taste reminds me of fathoms of bitter truth. I still marvel, still drink it in.

I never liked black coffee before, but I suppose my tastes have refined.

No Lock No Key.

The room of my heart will always be unlocked for you,

The light I leave on spilling under the door.

If you return you'll find me there, fluffing the pillows and smoothing the blankets. Turning around at the creaking of your footsteps to face the doorway.

I will not cry, refusing to contort my face with the accusatory, mournful lines of "how could you leave?"

Rather,

I will beam, happily softening my expression with the sweetest, gentlest, curves of "welcome back."

Creation Myth.

Give me a modicum and I'll turn it into miles and miles of reasons why-

Leagues and leagues of deeper meanings

Years and years of overspun conjecture in my mind.

Give me a but a dull moment and watch me turn it to technicolor-

A basic breath I could turn over in my hands, stretching and shrinking into soft song

A simple word I might run my eyes over till it blurs and becomes pages upon pages of them.

Anything is possible when your mind never stops working, never stops connecting and severing, never stops its conspiratory search for another pin to wrap its yarn around.

It's overactive, always overthinking until every thought to be had has been. Forming dreams and nightmares to layer atop reality, a haze of what if's and how about's.

Creating something out of nothing

That is my specialty.

Siena Mellor

Cry Baby.

My eyes are watering at least half of the time.

I feel like I harbor oceans behind my sclera, the whites of my eyes such a color from the sea foam that never stops washing over the windows of my soul.

I know, I know. To weep is not to be weak... but I can't help but feel small as I tumble in the seas of my own sorrow, washing my eyes out until they're puffy and red, lashes damply clumped together in solidarity.

But like the quiet shushing of waves crashing upon the shore, it seems the tears themselves murmur to my turbulent mind, a quiet whisper to bring me down from the high pitch of my whimpering as they slip down my face, like miniature surfers wiping out on the curves of my cheeks.

Shhh...

You can cry as long as you need,

Shhh...

Cry, baby.

Shhh...

Just cry.

Rock Bottom.

A pit that I seem to be rather well acquainted with.

In fact,

I have fallen to such depths so frequently

That my body's impact has begun to erode at the rock, a well-defined indent of myself forming in the hard surface of its floor.

I think maybe,

If I hit the bottomless bottom enough times,

I may fall through and meet Dante in his nine hells.

He'll take me to have a chat with the devil, so I can tell him to make his ceiling a little thicker next time.

That is,

If my skull doesn't split open and shatter the next time I dive headfirst into stone.

Reminder.

In...

Out...

Breath, the language of whispers. Soft shudders of the lungs drawing air

In...
and
Out...

I lay quiet, drowsy in the dark. More or less focused on the tell-tale sound of my own respiration.

I can imagine how my own chest looks with my eyes closed.

Feminine swells lifting up (*In...*)
Deflating back down (*Out...*)

Resting my hand upon it I feel the warmth of comforter covered skin, rising and falling with only so much as a snuffle. A quiet reminder in the black and blues of night that I am still alive.

I wonder if you ever remind yourself of your own mortality like this... Taking a mute note of your lung's oxygen exchange.

Do you ever have to remind your mind that you're still breathing, that you've yet to fade away into silence to the point of

No longer breathing (*In...*)
Becoming utterly snuffed (*Out..?*)

The shadow of death has yet to claim us.
But sometimes I need a physical marker to tell me so, to alert me to my own existence.

I hope you don't.

I hope you are so assured in your own life that you do not lie awake, counting each rise and fall, connecting every inhale to its exhale.

May you simply sleep, blissfully unaware of every draw

In...
and
Out...

Flavors.

Find someone who likes the same flavors you do.

Or else your cinnamon will clash with their spearmint, and the taste of each other's lips will seem incompatible with what lingers on your tongue.

The burn of spice you relish does not mix well with the cool of menthol.

So find someone who likes the same flavors, even if you could compromise with bubblegum instead.

Tenderly.

I trace my own neck.

Though the motion is a poor imitation of what I need,
My soft hands are no replacement for your calloused palms.

But I try to soothe myself anyway because

I am no longer safe,
No longer stable.

The lights are out and the door doesn't lock,
I am sitting in a house that doesn't
Belong to me anymore.
(Squatters rights I suppose.)

I feel displaced in every face I peer into.
They are all warped, features that betray humanity
but not their own sense of it.
It unsettles me,

So I disappear back into myself.

I read the sheet music you left behind in my memory.
The rhythm of my fingertips strumming along my jugular reminiscent of the song still playing in my heart.

Of all the things that I have had to let go of, this feeling will not be one of them. Even if I have to close my eyes and conjure up the air to fill my grasp in your stead.

Following the trail you blazed,

The path ingrained by our flesh's limerence

I trace my own neck.

Romance Section.

Love stories with second chances always were my favorite,
But sometimes life doesn't follow the storyline.

I Understand.

I understand that I am no longer needed here,

You have made this abundantly clear.

I know that as the years have gone by my presence is rendered increasingly obsolete,

There is no place for the outdated in your arms.

I understand this all perfectly, and yet I cannot *accept* it.

Just because I can comprehend that you don't want me like a fact doesn't mean I can know it like one.

I am past tense and you are future but both can exist in the same sentence can't they?

"She was foolish for believing he'd turn around, because he's going to keep on walking away." (I told you, see?)

I have stood here and waited like the fool Jay Gatsby *was* and Daisy Buchanan *wished* she could've been, hopeful for the flick of your gaze backwards while you keep it firmly forward. Intent on stepping into bright new eras without me.

I understood then

I understand now
I will keep understanding later

Yet this still doesn't change how I feel.
Logic cannot override my pathetic refusal of reason.

There is simply nothing I can do to change your mind.

But I will try anyway, and I'll keep trying until one day I break down like the redundant, out of date system I am and disintegrate into my very own Valley of Ashes. My resolve rusting away until all that remains is my comprehension of your fading footsteps and the dust of my desire to hear them come closer.

To the Ones That Come After.
(the ones I turn away)

I will look into your eyes and see someone I shouldn't

I don't text because he won't reply

I won't call because he doesn't pick up

I can't tell if he hates me or not

I don't know if I hate him or not

But none of that matters

Because you text and you call

I know you "love" me I don't have to debate

(you told me in three days and he told me in seven, I don't want to think about how flimsy a word it must be then.)

Who cares if your ways are crude and crass?

(His were always eloquent and beautiful)

It's fine. You're different.

(It will never be the same)

You aren't like him. Not at all.

(At least you text and call)

So I will keep looking into your eyes for now.

(Even though I will never stop looking for glimpses of him in them as well)

More.

I am meant for so much more than this life.

I lay in my bed and rot. I wake at four in the afternoon and feel as if a fog has rolled into my mind. I stumble through it and see nothing.

It takes hours more for me to get up, I lay and rot and stumble until my own body's feeble need for survival reminds me that my bladder exists and I'd rather empty it in its proper receptacle instead of in my sheets.

Sometimes I eat, usually I don't. Sometimes I do something worth doing, most of the time I just go right back to bed. It's too foggy to attempt much else, I can't do what I can't see right?

Yet I curse myself in the night for allowing life to rot away with me, my precious days and dim desires decaying in the grave of my bed. I hold them close to my emaciated heart. It reeks of rotten potential. The stench swirls with the fog. I sink deeper into my pillows, deeper into this remorseful state, I fall asleep.

I would like to wake up.

Honeyed Taurine.

Honeyed Taurine slides down my throat. I empty the garish can just as fast as I got it, the sharp caffeine starting to flow through my veins, swirling with my sluggish blood

Thoughts rush by.
Bouncing inside the walls of my skull. They scream at me to move, to walk, to get up and run, but my body stays in place; the new energy seemingly not enough to motivate me to do anything else except lay here and drip. (my life puddling at your feet. What do you see in me?)

My eyes are heavy.
They wish to close, to feel the comfort of blackness- of nothingness. My heart however beats wild, the previous harmony ruined by the battle between my internal and external. The caffeine had already gotten to my ichor but not my other systems. (Do you remember? Will you remember?)

The chemical currents pierce through my skin.
The furious energy searing me from within, splintering through my anatomy. My bones are tired and my muscles are sore as the honeyed taurine cracks through, splitting me open from the inside. I'm spilling out on the floor. (Can you feel the warmth? Can you feel the intensity? Can you feel the trembling untold inside of me?)

The unnecessary energy seeps from my pores.

Artificially flavored tears slip down my cheeks mixing with the honesty leaking from me.

My blood is not sluggish (It is afraid. Don't you see that?)

My body does not move, not because it is unmotivated (It clings to what it has, afraid of what it will lose once changed. Don't you know that?)

And all at once my life spilling out (before you) flows back into myself. The residue of what was once puddling left sticky and fluorescent. The open cracks and scars reform and heal themselves, sealing what was out (in front of you) back inside of me. The energy finally balanced between the internal and external.

My body moves (right beside you). My eyes slide shut and open again, blinking back those artificially flavored tears (they were your favorite flavor). The caffeine buzz equal at last in all my systems.

Giving me the euphoric energy to exist again, accepting my life has forever stained the floors we walk on

(Together).

Look at Me. (a question)

I keep asking the same question. A curiosity built of isolation, unrequited love, and an immense ache so unexplainable that it extends past my own consciousness deep into my psyche.

"What happens to the silent when words are left unsaid?"

...

What happens when all the strings start neatly tied, feelings free flowing within the threads, when they turn knotted and the current erratic, until finally it all unwinds into a crumpled mess of doubt?

What should you do when the ends justify the means, the bridges not quite burned but dangerous to cross, when the chaos and stress just become too much?

What did you do?

What did you decide was right?

(What have you done.)

I could ask you for a response with my words forever, couldn't I?

But the eyes have always been the windows to the soul, to the human heart, to the truth. Crystal clear and willing to relay the deepest connections with a glance.

\

They did. They used to.

My thirst for this damned answer is tearing me apart, I feel utterly psychotic, the tears born of this obscure, obsessive, frustration cascading down through these empty years, seeping in I hope. I vehemently pray.

So tell me, you I had called *inamoratos*, with eyes once so warm. Those eyes I still so fervently desire, along with your soft features I crave within my hands, the words left for dead on your tongue I wish had reached my ears, the feelings you drowned in ice.

I watched grieved as those dark irises of yours clouded with disillusionment, with the frigid nothing of those who are uncaring and unknowing. Your eyes now absent and full of fog.

Tell me what is supposed to happen? As I bore my gaze into that of the blind. As I grasp a fraying thread so hard that my nails dig crimson half-moons into my palm.

Even in your icy blindness your eyes are still beautiful, still hauntingly warm to me, they are not as inscrutable as you would have me believe.

(The falsity ingrained in human connection is inescapable when private longing is not reflected. But isn't it? Maybe I'm fooling myself, but your subtleties are not forgotten by me. I see as clearly as your gaze used to be the staring of your soul reflected in the unnoticeable.)

My desire for you has left me to be met with your own brevity, my skin engulfed alone by the cold we found solace beside each other in.

I can see the frustration that flickers inside you. Frustration that my insatiability is not shallow and fleeting but deep and piercing, I know you have attempted to placate me, quell my greed for the truth with half-answers and barely there conversations, they're enough to stall but not stop my search.

You're trying to make me quit. Trying to maintain that layer of ice over the deep waters of your heart. Trying to maintain the blizzard in your eyes while mine blaze with fire. I'm sorry that I haven't given up on you yet, I know it is inconvenient, but I am selfish and self interested in you.

Despite your avoidant efforts my question still remains unanswered. Your mouth stays a graveyard, your features maddeningly still, your ink black eyes reflecting an impenetrable frigidity.

"What happens to the silent when words are left unsaid?"

Do you know?

Or do I know you like I think I do?

Hold Hold Hold.

Everyone talks about moving on like it's this beautiful thing

A grand process of progress, "getting it together" as if the world will suddenly become vibrant again, the act of turning the saturation up so high you can't see the black and the grey of loss anymore. Everyone phrases it like it will change your life.

As if the grief hadn't already.

But nobody talks about the peace in holding on. Nobody wants to tell you about how they felt safer swaddling their hearts and minds in the hues of noir films, that foggy grey area obscuring everything in sight. Shielding them from that bright, bright world threatening to blind them with its unbearable color.

Nobody wants to talk about how comfortable it is to sink into pain. Letting it melt into your bones and spread its aching warmth through your chest. Like an old worn-in couch grief welcomes you, beckoning your tired, tear-stained body to relax into its cushions. It will not soften the blow, but it will always break your fall.

But most of all.

Nobody talks about how terrifying it is to let go. How scary it is to release the aches and the grey and the fog, nobody tells you about the fear that courses through your veins when you're about to let go of something that you so desperately sunk your claws into. Something that you can't bring yourself to stop holding close to your heart despite its breaking.

If you let go will there be something else to fill your empty hands?

If you let go what were all the aches and grey, and fog for?

If you let go what is left?

If you let go...

So I let go.

And it feels almost the same.

This description of releasing attachment you hear all the time makes it sound like it's an instant relief, like the second the words "I'm letting go" leave your lips the melancholy stored in your flesh will evaporate into warm fuzzy feelings again...

When has anything ever been that easy.

The only difference is that now you're no longer clutching desperately onto broken glass. Hoping, praying, that the blood being drawn from your pierced palm will somehow dry and hold what once was together again.

Instead, you look upon it from far away, broken shards of memory and pain glittering in the sun, enticing you to take the pieces into your hands again and squeeze, to add your ruby into the sharp odds and ends of glass once more.

But now you know better than to listen, one look at the scabs and scars covering your skin is a fearsome reminder of the price you pay for pain.

Still though. The dull throbbing in your flesh, it lingers. The temptation to take up the sparkling shards and slice yourself open, it tingles up through your nerves. That masochistic urge to return to the blood and the tears...

But like I said before. You know better, so you tear your gaze away and focus instead on the cool wind brushing through your loose hands.

The art of letting go, isn't always so much about the releasing. Sometimes it is about keeping your hands idly unclasped at your sides, and keeping your eyes anywhere else but on the litter of the past.

Constellation Complaint.

Attempting sleep is not easy, not when the stars exchange their grievances with me.

Billions of tiny voices building up to a whisper in my ear. Lamenting their dim light. A mere twinkling in the sky, "a lacking shine" they claim drearily.

I try to roll over, brush their whining off in hopes they will find another unlucky dreamer to bother. But they continue. They tell me of the moon and their jealousy.

"I wish her light was mine..." they all sigh. A silky mixture of adoration and resentment reaching my ears and rousing me from my indifference. Getting up I look out my window, eyes scanning across the billions of sad stars shimmering gloomily in the inky night.

My gaze skips over each of them, settling on a brighter shine peeking out from the clouds.

I see the moon.

I see the gentle glow about her, how she illuminates the ether, and I gasp. Pressing my hands against the glass, trailing the soft curve of her face with my eyes before she is obscured by the sky once more.

I retreat to my bed, back to the soft lulls of discontentment from the stars, only this time I feel a stirring in my chest. A whisper of understanding. Sympathy for the celestials I had paid little mind to.

I part my lips, letting syllables join the air that escapes me, my words joining this interstellar choir of dejection.

“I wish her light was mine.”

Hip Bones.

Thin hands tracing along, halting upon the knife-point of skeletal anatomy.
A reminder of the body's fragility;
The ilium of her hip bones timidly jutting out and away,
Sharp enough to slice, delicate enough to splinter with enough pressure.
Flesh formed of parchment, Musculature made from ribbon, and a mind modeled after mosaics.
But-
Her bones are built of glass, she is shatterable.
The most desired porcelain doll.
A crack resounds,
She smiles.

Hedonic/Ascetic.

Are you or are you not defined by your desires?

Such is a question from philosophy,

The paradox of discipline and freedom.

Something intangible in the mind, morphing into a graspable need.

Am I not my silent mouth and self control?

Or am I simply the carnal wails of my heart?

(Could we be both, must we be either)

Maybe I will be defined by one today and the next tomorrow.

A query forever ingrained in law and life.

I Made You a Martyr.

I made you a martyr.

A victim of my life, of my love
I look upon you with eyes glossed over in reverence, a saint who turns away from prayers and offerings of devotion. Candles lit, incense burned, my heart and mind on a silver platter. What should I have given you? What should I have placed upon your altar instead?

I made you a martyr.

You who once blessed me, made me priestess
I will sing hymns of your praise until my lips turn blue and the echo of my voice in these halls deafens me. I tend to the pews and pillars in this house of prayer without fail. But what good is a temple for divinity that deserts? What good can come from an empty place such as ours?

I made you a martyr.

This title suggests death, but you have found new life
I have breathed it into your corpse- a resurrection wrought of my selfish desire. Though you grace the earth only in my visions, dreams of futures we could have had. Is it really so vain to think they were prophecies? Is it wasteful of my soul to hope?

I made you a martyr.

And you will forever damn me for it.

Thunderstorms.

This is why I close my eyes.

For when I open them it is not the ceiling I am greeted with but the gentle glow of a dream. Even through REM, I can feel the corners of my mouth raise into a smile.

Because where I find dreams, I find you as well.

Tonight you've sat beside me as if it was the only place you wanted to be. Knuckles grazing mine so absently that one would think it was natural, the way things have always been.

Even in the distortion dreaming carries your face is still perfectly clear, my subconscious committing its construction to pristine memory. In fact, everything belonging to you; from the warmth of your body to the smell of your clothes seems realer than the morning I will undoubtedly wake up to.

Dark eyes draw my rapt attention back before your lips steal it, a bolt of surprise and ardent impulse rocketing through me,

I can feel it just as if I was awake. Just one kiss sending a fierce, searingly hot, striking of longing into my marrow, spreading throughout like little branches of blazing lightning, licking from my collarbone to my lungs. Stealing my breath away.

The look this illusory rendition of you gives me after tells me the same thunder must have rumbled in your chest. Faltering my heart in its steady rhythm and sending me inching closer, begging with the invisible that you too are reaching out for me.

I find that indulgent wish granted the moment another electrical storm explodes from your lips to mine. An overflow of energy sparking me to light just before the sunrise takes me away.

Leaving me gasping, wide awake with an erratic pulse and a chest full of hot thunderstorms.

Torrents.

The rain falls, an irregular pattern of persistence much like my own heartbeat. There are hurricanes in my head as I trail after your footsteps, your calculated gaze the eye of my storm.

My voice trembles in my mouth and the thunder rumbles louder. I can't tell if it is simply the sky or if I'm really crying, but the water falls faster all the same.

You stop and my world turns. The clouds gathering thicker than my throat as I swallow the syllables that threaten to flood the world around us, choking on gallons of words that would surely sodden the firm ground you stand on.

I know that I will drown in open air if I stay here. Cold winds stinging my skin and sheets of rain soaking through my clothes into my bones as I falter, for everything I am worth I hold back the hurricane raging in my chest, because I would rather slip silent beneath a stormy sea's surface than to speak and drag you under.

I can't let you feel the force of these conversations constrained within *my* lungs.

I can't allow you to become wet with *my* watery weaknesses.

I can't dampen your day with *my* torrential downpours.

Candy.

A candy coating of my person.

Thin layers of sugar to veil the bitterness harbored within my form, my insides dark with the disillusionment of life.

Getting greedy and crunching through only seems to disappoint those around me, where one expects sweetness they find only withered fruit and rot.

I'm sorry I am not what you thought I was.

I wish I could be sweet mallow through and through, your face twisted in sour contempt telling me all I need to know about your expectations. But didn't you see the shriveled decay behind the shine of my skin? Couldn't you tell?

I suppose that means I did a good job. Stretching ribbons of candied coverings to hide behind. You perceived something safe to eat, something easy to digest. But now you've found the core behind all that spun sugar.

I make you sick to your stomach.

why not me

To the Girl Who Wrote This in the Bathroom Stall.

I do not know, and I am sorry.

I wish I could tell you why you were not chosen.
Why you were not enough.
Why you were inferior in their eyes.

Sometimes having the answer is painful, more often having none is worse,

The never ending struggle of not knowing why you couldn't be... will always haunt you.

And I know this because it haunts me.
Because it haunts her.
Because it haunts him.

"Why not me." Is a question that just refuses to be answered.

Even when we deserve to hear it.
Even when they deserve to tell us.

But maybe, take into consideration what can be now that it is not you?

Think of the new dawns that will rise over the horizons of your heart, especially on the days you wish to sleep forever.

Think of the tides that will ebb and flow in your mind, carrying away the pollutants of doubt and replenishing your thoughts with fresh dreams to pursue.

It may not be you, but you can become something better, something that they will wish they had.

A new opportunity they will lament over missing.
A grand prize no one may win but yourself.

All because it was not you.

I Have Killed Myself a Thousand Times Over.

The suicidal ideation of change.

I can't stand the me that I am so I'll simply kill her and stitch a new person to be out of patchwork and the scraps that remain in my every reincarnation.

I find myself only as I carve my chest open, a vivisection of the heart.

I turn myself inside out, outside in, reorganizing organs and my thoughts in due time as my brain begins its paradoxical decomposition into something new.

Rotting away until the soil reforms me, a fresh body rising from the earth only to do it all over again-

The cycle goes on.

The circle of life has always been gruesome. Why should creating a new one for myself be any less just because I am human?

It does not matter how many times it takes, how many reiterations of resurrections are required to metamorphosize into someone I can be content living in the skin of. When given the choice between self-slaughter or shattered sanity, I will always take up the blade that will lead to my own actualization.

Avarice.

Avarice, the sin of greed. A creature I am most intimate with, for it whispers in my ear to take, take, take, all that could be mine. And when my plate is empty I will snarl and grasp for more, satisfaction a word I will never know.

It almost sounds like a name. Something I could shorten, turn sweet. The greedy devil on my shoulder sprouts feathery wings and a silky tone. Deplorable, horned Avarice donning the guise of simple drive, becomes the admirable, haloed Ava. Torn between perching on my right or left, she burrows into the divot of my sternum.

Is it my fault for never feeling full? It does not matter how many accolades I shovel into the depths of my throat, I feel as if I am starving, striving for something unachievable.

There must be something out there that I may take hold of, that I could swallow like a key and keep forever, locking the bottomless pit of my appetite closed.

I know that what I have is enough for someone like me, but the need to grasp beckons me so naturally. The feeling in my gut screaming that I must take hold of another new conquest, only to devour it discarding my decorum. Crunching down on my exploits like bird bones between my molars.

Is there something stuck in my teeth? Ava's asking.

Wishful Thinking.

I fear for my sanity in your absence.

My mind twists and turns in circles, turning memories over and over in my palm until every sharp corner is smoothed, wild jungles in my mind becoming well-worn trails, pathways I pave with my incessant pacing through them.

Though I ruminate in this skull waterlogged by memory and emotion with ease I know it is only brought from repetition, I know that the very fact of that is neurotic.

I sit with the past easier than I can stand the present. Sinking below the surface of what was and what could've been rather than facing what is.

It's reflexive. Just as one jumps back from a hot stove my thoughts jump back to you in moments of quiet. *Smoothing, Pacing, Sinking...*

If I had the choice would I empty my mind? If it was as simple as unscrewing the lid and pouring it all down the drain would I?

No. I'm too much a coward for an action as permanent as forgetting.

I know that in any effort to discard you wholly I would discard myself as well. Becoming much too heavy handed in the shaky spill of my mind, sending us both swirling down the pipes.

At least then there would be no sanity to fear for, as we would both be absent.

Oversteeped.

The tea gets bitter the longer it sits.
Soggy leaves bogged down with the weight of water and time swirl in their strainer, and yet I don't bother to remove them from the pot.

It's old porcelain china, a set from someone long passed. There is a crack running gracelessly down the spout and splintering off into the otherwise smooth circular surface.

When I pour a new cup the liquid dribbles from that black jagged gash, scattering wet droplets onto the table below. There are water spots staining the wood, evidence that this is not the first time I have used this pot and insinuating that it will not be the last despite its helpless dripping.

The tea gets bitter the longer it sits.
I know this, there is no reason for my nose to scrunch startled even when the next sip seems harsher to take than the last. The acrid flavor melts over my tongue and my nose scrunches anyways.

This does not stop me from raising the cup to my awaiting mouth again. I let my lips kiss the rim of the glass, warmed by my frequent indulgence of this atrocity. The steam perfumed with the scent of things past due.

A part of me will always wonder why I ruin my drinks this way. Sitting and sitting, steeping and steeping. Letting the liquid turn from pale to perfect to putrid.

The tea gets bitter the longer it sits.

Sunday.

Sunlight filters through the window I left open the night before, the cool breeze once lulling me to a soft slumber now carrying birdsong and the urge to rise.

The mornings where my head may raise slowly and my hands can keep their gentle grasp upon plush pillows are the mornings I can feel in my flesh.

I can't help but think that these are a blessing, a gift the earth gives after the week passes. As if the planet itself heralds the arrival of rest and ease.

Nuzzling deeper into my comforter as my thoughts begin to stir, everything down to my bones feels warm, the aches of yesterday long forgotten

There was a reason the Lord declared today the day of rest, a moment bestowed solely for the sake of recuperation.

It's finally Sunday.

To Clean a Steam Wand.

The ventures of my palm are met with steam that sears.

I have done this motion a million times before, and yet an angry blotch of burned skin howls at my nerves from its place on my hand.

I wonder how in my practiced repetition I have gotten it wrong today. And the further inflamed patch of flesh responds in its silent scream.

Carelessness.
When you have done something forever you lose caution, the discretion of beginners abandons you and in place pride takes hold.

The notion that I could get something so simple so wrong seemed impossible, and yet here I am, running the palm of my hand under cool water.

I still have to clean that wand.

Rosewater

Moon Jelly.

Jellyfish move by being pushed and pulled through the sea.

The forces of water drifting them along in the open ocean,

Delicate forms swirling in the directions provided to them.

I hope you understand when I call myself *moon jelly* then,

For all my soft body craves are the currents that will carry me

Gently back into your arms.

Present Tense.

There is no “ed” to love.

The words “I loved him” will never leave my lips. The suffix means only destruction, an end, as final as the stroke of an executioner's hands.

“I loved him” can only mean that I stopped. that the beating of my heart died the day he broke it.

And as much as it felt like death had taken hold of my pulse and clenched its fist back then, I found my heart still pounding in my cracked chest.

To say it beat for me, however, would be a bold face lie.

It only ever beats for him.

So even when I thrash and sob violently into the night, my voice will never choke on that suffocating syllable. Even when I am given no reason to hold on, I will not speak such a withered word.

Because there is no “ed” to love. Not if it’s true.

Musings

Siena Mellor

Annotated.

My most prized possession is a book entitled *Winter Roses After Fall* by Robert M. Drake and r.h. Sin. This copy was the first of many collections of poetry that have fallen into my possession. Though this didn't just drop into my eager hands, it was a gift. A token of affection bestowed to me by someone dear.

Usually when someone gives you something nice you put it up. Leave it untouched. Keeping the pretty thing pristine for fear that taking it in your hold for too long will wear it to bits... You love it from a distance.

But this was a book, and I love my books hard. Up close and personal, tossing it into every bag whether or not I think I'll be able to read it where I'm going. Opening it so fast that I crack the spine- way too excited for the chance to take in the words, letting my eyes scan the pages over and over again, going cover to cover only to flip right back to the beginning tomorrow to see what I didn't yesterday.

My favorite books all show a physical marker of my love. They look worn, well lived with, corners of paperback covers curling and pages losing their crisp edge. The most vivid display though, are the rainbow flurry of tabs sticking out from within the wisdom inside, little scribbles in the margins describing my thoughts, detailing emotions one stanza may elicit, underlining raw lines...

I love my books to the point of near memorization, my hands know every texture and imperfection on the paper's surface, the way the printer ink bled over there, how someone dog-eared the page in the middle long before this was bought for me. (I'm glad to know someone thought the words in my darling gift were important enough to make their own marker of.)

All of this to say, my most prized possession looks to be a little worse for wear.

I've overstuffed the margins, sticky tabbed near every page. I find something meaningful in every line, to me it's impossible not to note *something* down for it.

I've dragged it along on all my journeys, from serene beaches to smoggy cities. Traveling state lines, crossing countries through air. It's almost as if I am determined to make this little two hundred and thirty-three page collection of poems as well traveled as I. The memory of each trip is displayed in the integrity of its cover, its matte coating rubbing away in patches to reveal shiny paperboard. Creases in the paperback from when I let it jostle in my bags too long, my other belongings bending back its delicate cover leaving a permanent scar.

Perhaps there is something to be said about loving from a distance. Despite how I love my books, the way I love people is different. More restrained, I put them up on pedestals in my head, adoring from afar, hands itching to hold and carry with me everywhere but never reaching out. A mind burning to know more than I allow myself to ask, and share more than I can get to slip from my mouth. All because I don't want to break them.

While cracking the spine of a book in eager anticipation is fine, I fear I'll crack a heart with my impulsivity. Dragging my copies along with me is a lot less terrifying than dragging someone along though my ups and downs hoping they don't get too damaged.

Sometimes I look at my dear copy and feel sorry for it, that the price of my affection has marred its original perfect form. Other times I recall that besides being known (and god is this book known by me) being loved also means that you will be changed. Shaped by the people and their influence around you.

I see the prism of colored tabs fluttering in the breeze while I'm reading outside, I let my eyes scan the matte patches turned glossy. They look almost like stars swimming in the cream of the cover. This visual representation of my adoration makes me feel light, happy that I can see the lines of my appreciation.

Change ultimately is good, and maybe I might have to start loving my people like my books, bending back the covers even if it hurts for a moment, highlighting their presence in my life, and sticking tabs along each and every moment together. Finding a way to stop fearing the possible scars of the rough patches to enjoy the gloss of what may lie underneath. Knowing that since change is certainly along the way, so is a mutual knowing. I'd rather memories and deeper connections settle into the lines of a relationship well annotated instead of dust coating someone I've fearfully left untouched.

Nihilistic.

To be void of meaning.
Such is nihilism.

I have been told that my work is "nihilistic" in nature, and a part of me agrees. Dismantling the simplistic preconceived notions of love and hatred as if they meant nothing is a part of my obsession, an ideology I spew with the ease of breath.

Yet I find the term an insult.

Because to call my poetry nihilistic is to assume that I am simply stating that these feelings and ideas **actually** mean nothing. That there is no true substance behind them.

A thought that is at heart, ridiculous.

Human beings crave simplicity,
We crave the thought of everything being simple enough to shove into cardboard. Each facet of life must fit into every flimsy box the mind constructs because when things are simple they are **controlled**.

And if something is controlled it usually has no substance. It has nothing besides what the controller allots.

The thought that anything could be more than black and white unsettles the brain.

Unfortunately, I am of the firm opinion that most things are painted in vibrant color, and consist of ever-shifting forms. Something a box just can't contain.

So when people say that my work is "nihilistic" I hope what they really mean is that what I find meaningless is humanity's constant endeavor to constrain forces such as love and hatred to simple rules, standards, and formulas.

I could never in good conscience say that there is no meaning. I'm saying there is meaning beyond what we may comprehend.

I hear the way people trivialize these things and make them something base to kick around, terms like "situationship" or "ick" make me ill. How is it that feelings so powerful can be squeezed and compressed into something of a commodity? Are people not overcome with enamorment anymore? Are the quirks of others no longer endearing and now something to wither at?

"The three month rule", "if they wanted to they would", "ghosting", the list goes on and on. Ignoring the unique contexts and complications of relationships in favor of shoving human behavior into generalized categories rids such connections of their respective flourish on our soul.

The real void is found in our efforts to seal these things to a trend, a time, or a type. This is true nihilism.

"Grief is just love with no place to go."

-Jamie Anderson

One day I walked into an in-person session of my poetry class and was struck through the temples with this quote.

Tommy Domino, my mentor and no stranger to grief himself, let the words slip from his lips like truth from scripture, and I found that it resonated deeply with me, as if I had held this belief before knowing its verbal construction.

Despite only being 17 as of writing this, I have my own deep relationship with grief, and I would venture to say that you, the person reading this, do as well. It is a universal experience; yet another bitter flavor of human existence.

Grief is a genre of sadness that differs from its siblings though, because grief is specifically born of subtraction, brought forth in one from *losing* someone dear to them, rather than being thrust into a new complication.

However, I have found that people tend to always associate grief with death. While an understandable connection to draw I think this is a meaningless constraint, as the loss of a friendship or a relationship garners the same feeling. A casket is not necessary for someone to be truly lost to you, someone's hand pulling away from your own can be just as final as the rattling of a last breath.

I wonder which form plagued Jamie Anderson when she put her pen to paper and divulged this thought, sometimes I wonder which plagues me to the point that her words have lived in my marrow for so long.

Was it the death of my grandmother? The beginnings of grief that I will carry numbly beside fuzzy memories of Disneyworld and a florally wallpapered nursing home...

Was it the scorn of old friends? Ripping up the roots of our shared childhood to plant themselves elsewhere. Shaking my soil and teaching me to be okay with growing inward instead...

Or maybe it could've been the loss of a lover? Although I find that that particular loss brings with it more than grief. An absurdly large amount of more...

A much likelier possibility is that they all swirl together, different shades of missing persons melding into a drab grey to shade my soul with. Grief is not the only color within my aura, yet it is ever present. Sometimes it lingers like the soft snuffling that accompanies air in breath. Other times it slams into me much like a truck running a red light, unforgiving and forceful.

If grief has no place to go, then that insinuates that it either circulates through me alongside the blood in my veins, or that it bleeds out into my surrounding life; seeping into the intricacies of my interactions. A paradoxical attachment in either case, considering how it is created. Love with no destination turned sorrowful through its harboring.

This isn't to say of course that grief is unbearable, that it overpowers with its burden on one's already heavy shoulders, like a shadowy mirror of how love is felt wholeheartedly, its uplifting sensation buzzing within every cell in regards to whomever it is directed. Grief may begin with such power, like an insurmountable wave keeping you crushed. Drowning flat against the floor underneath its weight.

Yet as the time passes after losing that guardian-friend-lover-etcetera, the tides become less oppressive, less overbearing, regressing from a tsunami to a gentle lapping at your ankles. And while the surrounding air may be tinged with sea spray, a deep inhale shows not only that you can keep your head above water, but that you can breathe again.

A Message to the Gentle. (strength)

To be gentle is a quality that has been ground away by the raw edges of our society, like flesh constantly rubbing against a cinder block edge. Gentleness has been skinned under the guise that it is a quality representative of the weak.

As I get older, I find it becomes a conscious effort to refrain from slipping into harshness. In any context of interaction my words on more occasions than I would like to admit have come out curt and blunt. I seem to have an affinity for becoming sharp and unforgiving with those around me and even myself so it is a constant effort to keep such tendencies in check.

I strive to do so because contrary to societal belief, I know intimately that gentleness is a hallmark of strength.

To many that statement is laughable, as the two are commonly perceived antonyms of one another, possibly complete opposites. In this world, the idea of strength has been contorted to represent aggression and the ability to be unapologetically self-serving; even to the point of cruelty. This caricature is in part brought to us by basing our expectations solely on figures of raw physical prowess instead of in tandem with figures of emotional intelligence.

Why is this a problem? Is it not the ones who can force their opposition into submission that rule the world? Is it not the ones who can bite the hardest and growl the loudest that rule the animal kingdom? Predators are the perceived conquerors of the day in their environments, all sharp teeth and sharp claws. So why would our society be any different, simply because those teeth and claws shift into brutish bodies and the ability to berate?

This adoration of "assailation" is face value. A shallow, materialistic view of what it means to be strong based on action movie stars and war stories. Now, there is nothing inherently wrong with the desire to be physically adept, or to have respect for the harsh realities of life and the cruel interactions that are sometimes necessary, but to idolize these facets as the ***only*** markers of strength brings fault.

I have heard on more than one occasion that being gentle is a trait belonging only to the demure, often also being relegated to being a solely feminine feature of the personality.

I would like to refute this idea.

Gentleness is a trait that reveals itself in somewhat similar fashions in regard to behavior amongst men and women, but that has entirely different rippling effects in both sexes.

In the minds of women, the idea of gentleness may make some of us cringe. Despite my defense of it now, I understand that such a nature is expected, and has been groomed into many of us from a young age in accordance with the stereotype of a "soft submissive girl." However, I will ask the feminine readers here to pause and consider that gentleness is not what makes us the perceived Lolita of Nabokov's world, nor does it make us any less than. It is rather the idea that gentleness cannot coexist with authority that has poisoned its merit, and this is in my opinion wrong.

In fact, when translated to the masculine among us, that possibility for coexistence becomes blatantly apparent. I firmly believe that a man with a gentle manner will always be more powerful and commanding than a man with an iron grip or fearsome speech. Simply because I have had the opportunity in my life to have experienced both in several different scenarios and relationships.

Each man is determined to make his word law, but depending on their nature each left an entirely different inscription in my mind. The ones who grabbed with the intention to bruise, to swing and crack bone, to raise his voice to raise hell. Their reflections in the pools of my eyes will always come back revealing a coward, one with no true means or ability to communicate. If violent reckoning is all he can bring then, regardless of his position- be it a father, a brother, a lover, a friend-, he becomes a crack in the foundation of every home he inhabits, the weakest link, a chain perpetually rusting.

Whereas with the ones who speak soft and touch softer, I would follow to the ends of the earth and frequently do. Simply because they display control of themselves and the impulse to fight. They would rather guide my hand and gaze than force them. In an age where the loudest and meanest are all anyone wants to be, the quiet and sweet become invaluable to those like myself who are tired of covering our ears and cowering.

In a baser, more animalistic comparison, society's identification of gentleness is with delicate meek lambs. *Prey.* Their soft nature is forced upon them by their lack of claws and sharp teeth, not by an intrinsic tendency toward being so. This is not true gentleness. Rather this is frailty, the distinction found simply because it is not voluntary. That can be discovered in the wolves, in seeing that just as they can slaughter and shred with their claws and jaws, they may also carry their young by the scruff and lick at the wounds of their pack with the very same maw, all without drawing a drop of blood. They make the decision to be soft, not because they have to, but because they can.

True gentleness (and in turn true strength) come from making the choice to be.

So whoever you are, and whatever your circumstance, *never* let anyone tell you that your rounded edges are your fault. Shake your head when they tell you that softness is insufficient. Your gentleness is your strength, shielding you and the ones you love from the shrapnel of explosive arguments and binding together the ties that sharp tongues would sever.

Being *gentle* is synonymous with being *strong.*

Longing.

Love led lunacy.
That is the heart of what longing is.

To be honest, longing for something (anything really) is a truly humbling experience. It will bring you to your knees, and then unsatisfied with that, shove your face further into the dirt. All while simultaneously waxing its romantic sweet song through your veins.

You won't even taste the mud in your mouth because this feeling overpowers the senses of basic common sense. Heating your skin and fogging up your vision with the hue of roses one day, then turning you frigid and pricking tears in your eyes with their thorns the next.

With the modern introduction of short lived, instant gratification and dopamine hits, to long for something seems odd. Why wish for something you can't have when you could just keep scrolling, or find a substitute?

Because imitation has always been a failing form of flattery. To seek a substitution is just admitting you want that specific thing more. And when you get that sub-par selection you'll find yourself unable to settle with it.

Be it a place and your senses will feel ill at ease, **this house just isn't your home.**
Be it a taste and your mouth will feel revolted, **this flavor just isn't your favorite.**

Be it a person (*oh god be it a person.*) and your body will reject theirs, **they just aren't them.**

Longing for a person is out of any of the things to long for, the most brutal. No matter what you do, it will chase you down, unrelenting, and tear at your soul.

Try to forget? You'll certainly try, but the touch of another will make you nauseated. Distractions will never work, every store will undoubtedly have something they would like, every movie or art piece evoking memory. Music... Please, spare yourself that venture to another painful dead end. There is nothing to do but reside alone with yourself. Ruminating in your room with six pints of ice cream and a head heavy with wishes made too late.

Longing is a cruel mistress, cooing soft sweet things as she cuts you open. The nights alone are unbecoming, the hollow idea of going on like this will wear your mind to mere threads of thought. It feels visceral, like the sensation of starvation. Yet, to long is undoubtedly beautiful.

There is something definitively divine in the desiring of someone *untouchable* to your fingertips, like a sinner's spirit aching for God. Suffering, if done correctly, is religious in its own right.

Because longing signifies something unsettled in the soul, a chasm in your chest beckoning you to jump the ledge and plummet down. It's that nocturnal sort of pull, the kind that plagues insomniacs with the restless need to gather the bags under their eyes and sit in the night's silence. Ultimately you will jump. You will jump and plummet and break open. The blood pooling at your feet becoming the ink you scrawl their missed likeness upon the page with, the paint you use to grace a canvas with the honor of their form, the inspiration to exist on with some semblance of them even if you are truthfully without.

Longing is the driving force that brings you to meet a different kind of muse, an introduction to a mournful, masterful beauty. Longing will guide you to the feet of shared memories and sobs turned molten with desire only to instruct you to imbue your wounded heart into every printed letter and brush of acrylic.

"I pour myself out unto paper, ink flowing forth from my veins, my tears morphing into watercolor, yet it is always your eyes that look back, not mine."

This is the mantra of longing, to drive you mad to the point of obsessive creation. Filling you up with the desire to grasp what was once had, only to have you reach for an empty journal and write. It will not lessen the pain, but it will make it something manageable, an ethereal purge on the page, lest you let your emotions destroy you. Your pain bruising purple and hopes tinted pink become a tangible written world of impossible soft conversation and fantasy, alongside hardened confrontation of truth and reality.

Even if you never tell them how you ache for their hand in yours, the letters you leave behind in your tearful wake will always be a testament to your heart.

Longing.
The power of love *led* to lunacy.

Lonely.

"Self isolate and become unrecognizable in two months."

YouTube tells me this like it is a solution.

My algorithm presenting me with the array of faceless models panned across the thumbnail, each the spitting image of perfection.

I wanted to laugh at this, but the only thing I did was shut my laptop and look at myself in the mirror

Darkening purple bags hung low under my eyes, my skin was pale, my lips were cracked. I think back to the video my feed so proudly provided, and I feel my hands clench into weak fists.

Unrecognizable is right,
I look like hell.

I started to laugh then, and I kept laughing. I kept on letting laughter shake my body until the sound changed, contorting into sobs that choked me until I could just barely whimper. My hands covered my mouth as if I was going to be sick.

I sure felt sick. Sick to the very bottom of my stomach that I had let myself degrade away for so long.

And because of what exactly?

I'd argue that maybe it had just been a rough month, a depressive dip into the pools of fading away. Disappointed, disassociated, and distant.

The feeling of frustration and sadness soon dissolved back into apathy, almost as quickly as it came, and I laid back down, vaguely interested in how the damp skin of my face tightened ever so slightly as the tear tracks dried.

I thought with that same vague interest about how I've been hiding away, shying from others.

I roll over.

I've never been good with stress, my anxiety liked to spill out of my head and splash onto those around me, so maybe staying away looked like the better option. Keeping peace of mind for others seemed easier than keeping my own.

But even so, humans are social creatures. Isolation is damaging. It's true that you can be in the middle of a crowd of thousands, yet still be alone. No matter how I tried to swing it to myself, I craved the feeling of being with people, not simply just around.

Loneliness is a slow working poison, and often despite all best efforts and intentions it blooms in our heads, ensnaring our thoughts, our hearts, our lives...

You find yourself shutting down, shutting up.

Losing your appetite, losing your drive.

Your days become blurs, your nights not much better.

Ugh.

I clawed at my ears as if that would turn my idle musings down and roll over again. Unaware that in doing so I've just kicked my laptop off my mattress and onto the floor, gracelessly bruising my foot (and from the way the thud of the device sounded,) quite possibly my bank account.

Hearing the clatter I curse, get up, and check to see if I just cost myself several hundred dollars. Once I'm satisfied with finding no damage I look from my messy bed to the door, wondering if maybe instead of sleeping at five pm I should go outside...

I spare another glance at my computer, the screen is black but I can still picture that stupid thumbnail taunting me. Sneering at my sorry state. From the downward curl of my lips and furrowed brow, I can tell my glance just turned into a glare.

I grab my keys and slip out the door, deciding right then and there that these next two months I'll try to reconnect with some friends, eat better, sleep more.

Maybe I don't want to be unrecognizable,
Maybe I just want to feel like myself again.

Acknowledgements I

-To My Mother

My mother, wow. How do I possibly go about thanking someone who has sacrificed and poured herself into me since conception? You've been cultivating me in ways that strengthen, keeping me upright in my walk through life even throughout the terrors of this world that have threatened to tear me down. You always say that you'll "*never give me up to society*" and while at the time that phrase struck me as odd, now I am grateful for the way you have so fiercely protected me. As I grow up you have always put yourself to the side to take care of me first and foremost, even when I didn't deserve it. As I have grown not only as a young woman but also as an artist you have always shown your support for my work. Reading through my manuscripts back when they were messy piles of notes and unorganized printer paper, offering constructive criticism, and helping me pick a title that was not as arduous to read as the first five renditions. You've cradled me simultaneously in your arms and in your creative influence, all under the loving eyes of God. A simple acknowledgement is not enough, so I have further written your mark on me thus far the only other way I know how. A poem.

My Honor.

A mother, that of which God had blessed me with. The gentle touch of your firm hand striving to lead me down paths of which are brushless and easy.

You do all you can to pluck the thorns from my side when I stray and roll in briers, even as I bleat to bleed.

No amount of hardship has ever shaken you from your care of me, in my most tumultuous storms you are a lighthouse, guiding me to soft shores.

I dream of a day when I might return the favor, pay back my infinite dues to your duty, a future where we sit together and know rest.

You will laugh with ease and I will too. The briers turned to blossoms, the storms soothed, peace the only thing punctuating the sentences that make up the stories we will write of one another.

My adoration of you will never die, my lifeline tied to yours with the beat of love. It is my honor to call you mom, and may God never let me forget that.

I love you.

-To My Father

Dad, you know intimately how hard I've worked on this book and you've been there every step of the way. Our drives to Long Beach for my meets with my chapter will always be one of my most cherished memories of this time spent learning and writing. I can't thank you enough for the way you let me rattle on and on in the passenger's seat as I read you nearly the entire book, seeking your input and advice, things that you readily gave lifting me to greater heights in my work within those thirty-minute segments of our Saturdays together. Even before this though you were priming me for literary greatness. I distinctly remember the time you spent reading to me in any spare second life afforded, teaching me vocabulary and helping me sound out lengthy words my soft squishy toddler brain couldn't quite comprehend yet. I look back on all our deep conversations spent on discussing the merit of classics ranging from the likes of Fitzgerald to Nabokov, on poems I have written after hearing an odd word right out of Webster's drop from your mouth (words like *Detritus, Avarice,* shrapnel...) I know you tell me that I surpass you as a writer, but I wouldn't be at this level if it wasn't for you letting me step upon your shoulders. Like Mom, I find that for everything you have instilled within me from infancy to near adulthood this acknowledgement is simply not enough, so below is you immortalized, within the page.

The Strongest Man.

Your hands are calloused with the work of many years,

Skin hardened by the effort of scraping and clawing to success, to heights that befit you.

Your eyes betray the effort and sacrifice behind where you stand, the shadows of each version of yourself long past stretching behind the man you are today.

And yet,

The day I was born those rugged calloused hands became soft, the warmth behind your eyes betraying not just a man but a father. The shadow of who you were before me peering over your shoulder to coo at the newborn in your arms and to whisper well wishes and worries into your ear as you shifted into yet another new man.

To the strongest man I know, to the father I have been blessed with, thank you.

Thank you for your calloused hands that have guided me through every stage of my life.

Thank you for the long lectures and messages that remind me that like you I can achieve what seems impossible,

Thank you for the struggle and strife behind your eyes to be better than you were yesterday, all for the sake of raising me.

You are my father, the quiet strength I find within myself when I feel I could just shatter,

I love you.

Acknowledgments II

Siena Mellor

-To the Long Beach Chapter

To the Long Beach Chapter of CLI, thank you. When I first joined this group of talented poets, I never expected to find such a community. Every person I have met through this experience has left such a profound impact on my life, my heart, and my work. Between sharing critique during all of the workshopping and sharing doughnuts at the Long Beach public library every moment with this seasons Chapter has been a cherished one. I want to thank you all for teaching me how to utilize my words and materialize them beyond the page into my world. Without everyone I have had the privilege to work beside, this book would not ever have been possible.

-To Mrs. Miyadi

Mrs. Miyadi, from the moment I stepped into your English class freshman year I knew that I was going to love it. You made me feel welcome in my new environment and managed to spark a light not just in my passion for literature but one for poetry, that unit in class opening my eyes to an entirely new art form I had never even touched prior to that first assignment. I discovered a new world within the walls of your classroom, one that no matter my mood, or state of mind I could thrive in. No matter what, a piece of my success will always rightfully belong to you. (My first true work *Honeyed Taurine* was first penned in your class, after all.) When you asked me for an advanced reader's copy to say I was ecstatic would be a massive understatement, your motivation and genuine care for me as your student set me ablaze with the desire to start writing with the intent to never stop, and now here I am with a whole book! I cannot thank you enough for your presence in my life and the imprint you have left on it. You will always be my favorite teacher, one of UNI's best guiding hands, and in my eyes my most influential friend.

-To Mrs. King

Mrs. King, as someone who has been told for the better half of my few years on this planet that I was *more* than proficient in my writing, I want to first thank you for delightfully proving me wrong. I was skilled only in the literary artfulness of analyzing classics and waxing on and on upon pages I turned canvas, not in the skilled precision that is rhetorical writing. Through your class I have learned how to write in ways designed to swoon the college board but also coincidentally how to take aim upon any point I am trying to get across and hit the mark. Every class period providing experience I can use to sharpen my stanzas into blades cutting through meaninglessness. I will always be thankful for the instructional minutes you devoted to me in my 5th period. Additionally, though, the second thing I want to thank you for is how hard you worked to connect with me there. I felt seen for more than a student, and talking about the latest novels we've read and sharing a laugh will always be something I hold dear. I never had to worry when I would take certain poems or parts of the musings that have made their way into this book to you, because you always treated them with the same tender honesty you treated me with and that is something I will never forget.

About the Author

Siena Mellor is a teenage poet who can't leave a pen alone for the life of her. Perpetually walking around with ink stains on her skin she can be seen cuddling up with her cats, having five lattes too many, and roaming bookstores till they close. All while striving to pour her heart out onto everything she touches. Rosewater is her first book of many and her official debut into the poetry scene.

www.ingramcontent.com/pod-product-compliance
Lightning Source LLC
LaVergne TN
LVHW010935110826
845149LV00013B/2610
9798988458340